Sinatra
SET TO MUSIC

T0078490

PLAYBACK+
Speed • Pitch • Balance • Loop

To access audio visit:
www.halleonard.com/mylibrary

Enter Code
6005-7114-7626-2560

ISBN 978-1-59615-243-4

EXCLUSIVELY DISTRIBUTED BY

Visit Hal Leonard Online at
www.halleonard.com

Contact Us:
Hal Leonard
7777 West Bluemound Road
Milwaukee, WI 53213
Email: info@halleonard.com

In Europe contact:
Hal Leonard Europe Limited
42 Wigmore Street
Marylebone, London, W1U 2RN
Email: info@halleonardeurope.com

In Australia contact:
Hal Leonard Australia Pty. Ltd.
4 Lentara Court
Cheltenham, Victoria, 3192 Australia
Email: info@halleonard.com.au

One of the exciting challenges in music is learning to play a melody in the most musical, interesting, and personal way. This applies to both classical and pop music, giving the performer an opportunity for individual interpretation that is the essence of self-expression. Popular music offers us an especially broad latitude in this regard. The format presented here gives the instrumentalist a chance to play some of the loveliest popular melodies ever written. There are examples of playing straight melody, phrasing in such a way that the beauty of the composer's original concept is made quite clear to the listener. There are also examples where the performer plays a variation of the melody in such a way as to make it his own, giving a reading that is highly personal. The freedom in choosing which way to go, or perhaps combining both interpretations, is a feature that makes this kind of approach exciting.

These arrangements were originally written for singers, and it is refreshing to play these tunes in singers' keys since it takes us to places we would not ordinarily go. I hope that, ultimately, these songs with their harmonic structures will be so mastered by the player that they can be performed from memory in a variety of keys. If playing jazz is one of your interests, hearing familiar intervals in different keys is best for developing flexibility. It's great not only to loosen up this way, but there is no better method for ear training. Playing in uncommon keys also creates the possibility of using more interesting colors, and it challenges us to expand our technical capabilities. All of our musical lives should not be limited to the keys of C, F, and G.

You may recognize these arrangements since they were written for the likes of Frank Sinatra and Tony Bennet, so we're in good company. Listen, learn, play, and above all, have fun.

—Ron Odrich

CONTENTS

Ron Odrich

Ron Odrich is a clarinetist who has played and recorded with Clark Terry, Zoot Sims, Al Cohn, Phil Woods, Buddy De Franco, and other jazz greats. He has participated, teaching and playing jazz clarinet, in the Robert Marcellus Master Class at Northwestern University for twelve years. In May of 1992, he was featured as the first jazz artist to perform for the Scotia Festival of Music in Halifax, Nova Scotia. He has played in various New York City clubs, appearing weekly with his own quartet for the past thirty-five years. John S. Wilson, music critic of the *New York Times*, said Odrich is "recognized by fellow musicians as a jazz bass clarinetist virtually without a peer" and that he is "a brilliant jazz clarinetist…" His first album was with jazz greats Vinnie Burke and Chris Connors in 1955. His album, *Blackstick*, was given a four-star rating by *DownBeat* magazine.

Odrich is virtually a native New Yorker. Born in Connecticut, his family moved to the Empire State when he was very young, and he has remained in one or another of the five boroughs of New York City since then. His father, Jim, was an early mentor; he was originally a 'cellist who later doubled on the reeds and played saxophone, clarinet, and oboe in radio and recording studios and in many Broadway musicals. Odrich's first instrument was 'cello, but he switched to clarinet when he was thirteen years old after hearing the opening cadenza to "Rhapsody in Blue." His teachers, Sal Amato, Vincent Abato, Buddy DeFranco, Kalmen Opperman, Robert Marcellus, Daniel Bonade, and Lennie Tristano represent a "Who's Who" of virtuosic clarinetists.

Early club dates through the late '40s were followed by the Air Force Band "Airmen of Note," 1951–'53, and performances as part of the Vinnie Burke Quartet, Clark Terry (small and large) orchestras, on-stage acting/playing in the original Broadway cast of *Lenny*, and formation of his own quartet in the early 1980s.

Ron is also a periodontist with his own practice in Manhattan. Both his quartet and his dental practice were one of the feature stories on the August '94 Charles Kurault Show on CBS "Sunday Morning." He has also appeared on "Around New York" on station WNYC in '94 with a trio.

He was featured as a soloist at Carnegie Hall in the Memorial Concert for composer Morton Gould on March 20, 1996.

Ron performs on a regular basis with his group in one of New York's jazz clubs in mid-town.

Yesterdays

Music by Jerome Kern
Lyrics by Otto Harbach

Body And Soul

Bb INSTRUMENT

Lyrics by Edward Heyman,
Robert Sour, & Frank Eyton
Music by Johnny Green

Body And Soul

Bb INSTRUMENT

Fly Me To The Moon

Words and music by
Bart Howard

Pg. 8

It Was A Very Good Year

Bb INSTRUMENT

Words and music by
Ervin Drake

Orchestra

Speak Low

Words by Ogden Nash
Music by Kurt Weill

Speak Low

Angel Eyes

Words by Earl Brent
Music by Matt Dennis

That's All

Words and music by
Alan Brandt & Bob Haymes

rubato
1st time Slowly and freely
2nd time at Tempo

I can on-ly give you love that lasts for - ev - er, and the
on-ly give you coun - try walks in spring-time, and a

prom - ise to be near each time you call; and the on - ly heart I own, for
hand to hold when leaves be - gin to fall; and a love whose burn - ing light, will

you and you a - lone, That's All, That's All. I can
warm the win - ter night, that's

All, that's all. There are those I am sure who have

told you they would give you the world for a toy. All I

have are these arms to en - fold you and a love time can nev - er de -

stroy. If you're won - d'ring what I'm ask - ing in re - turn dear, you'll be

glad to know that my de - mands are small: say it's me that you a - dore, for

now and ev - er more, That's All, That's All.

Steppin' Out With My Baby

Words & music by
Irving Berlin

step- pin out___ with my ba - by Can't go wrong___ 'cause I'm in right___
Step- pin' out___ with my hon - ey Can't be bad,___ it feels so good___
Step- pin' out___ with my ba - by Can't go wrong___ 'cause I'm in right___

it's for sure,___ not for may - be That I'm all dressed up to-night!___
Nev - er felt___ quite so sun - ny
Ask me when___ will that day___ be?

And I keep on knock- in' wood!___ there'll be smooth sail - in' 'Cause I'm trim - in' my

sails___ With my top hat___ and my

white tie___ and my tails!___

The big day may be to- night!___

If I seem to scin-ti - late it's be-cause I've

Steppin' Out With My Baby

Prisoner Of Love

Bb INSTRUMENT

Words & music by Leo Robin, Clarence Gaskill and Russ Colombo

Prisoner Of Love

Embraceable You

Bb INSTRUMENT

Words by Ira Gershwin
Music by George Gershwin

Here's That Rainy Day

Words and music by
Johnny Burke &
Jimmy Van Heusen

MORE GREAT CLARINET PUBLICATIONS FROM

Music Minus One

CLASSICAL PUBLICATIONS

Advanced Contest Solos for Clarinet, Volume 1
Brahms • Hindemith • Mozart
Performed by Stanley Drucker
Accompaniment: Judith Olson, piano
Book/Online Audio
00400630...........................$14.99

Also available:
Advanced Clarinet Solos, Volume 2
00400321 Book/Online Audio...............$14.99
Advanced Clarinet Solos, Volume 4
00400322 Book/CD Pack.......................$14.99

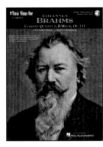

Johannes Brahms – Clarinet Quintet in B Minor, Op. 115
Performed by Collete Galante
Accompaniment: The Classic String Quartet
Book/Online Audio
00400323 ....$19.99

Johannes Brahms – Sonatas for Clarinet and Piano, Op. 120
No. 1 in F Minor &
No. 2 in E-Flat Minor
Performed by Jerome Bunke
Accompaniment: Hidemitsu Hayashi, piano
Book/2-CD Set
00400046.......................$19.99

The Clarinetist
Classical Pieces for Clarinet and Piano
Performed by Anton Hollich
Accompaniment: Harriet Wingreen, piano
Book/2-CD Set
00400122 ....$14.99

Clarinet Solos
Weber – Concertino, Op. 26 & Beethoven – Trio No. 4, Op. 11
Performed by Keith Dwyer
Accompaniment: The Stuttgart Festival Orchestra
Book/Online Audio
00400605.......................$19.99

W.A. Mozart – Clarinet Concerto in A Major, KV 622
Performed by Denitza Lavchieva
Accompaniment: Tempi Concertati Chamber Orchestra
Book/Online Audio
00400047 ....$19.99

W.A. Mozart – Quintet for Clarinet and Strings in A Major, KV581 "Stadler"
Performed by Keith Dwyer
Accompaniment: The Cassini Ensemble
Book/Online Audio
00400314..........................$19.99

Robert Schumann – Fantasy Pieces, Op. 73 & Three Romances, Op. 94
Performed by Jerome Bunke
Accompaniment: Hidemitsu Hayashi, piano
Book/Online Audio
00400316.......................$14.99

Carl Maria von Weber – Clarinet Concerto No. 1 F Minor, Op. 73 & Carl Stamitz – Concerto No. 3 in B-Flat Major
Performed by Keith Dwyer
Accompaniment: Stuttgart Festival Orchestra
Book/Online Audio
00400586.......................$19.99

POP/STANDARDS

Play the Music of Burt Bacharach
Performed by Tim Gordon
Accompaniment: The Jack Six All-Star Orchestra
Book/CD Pack
00400636 ....$14.99

Sinatra Set to Music
Performed by Ron Odrich
Accompaniment: The Al Raymond Orchestra
Book/Online Audio
00400711.......................$14.99

JAZZ/SWING

From Dixie to Swing
For Clarinet &
Soprano Sax
Performed by Kenny Davern
Accompaniment: The Dick Wellstood All-Stars
Book/Online Audio
00400613..........................$14.99

New Orleans Classics
Performed by Tim Laughlin
Accompaniment: Tim Laughlin's New Orleans All Stars
Book/Online Audio
00400024 ....$19.99

Swing with a Band
Performed by Tim Gordon
Book/Online Audio
00400637 ....$14.99

What Is This Thing Called Jazz?
A Jazz Man's Approach to Great Standards
Performed by Ron Odrich
Book/CD Pack
00400681 ....$14.99